Quick Guide to CV Building, Job Search and Interview Skills

Employability Skills

Isiak A. Sanusi

Quick Guide to CV Building, Job Search and Interview Skills –

Employability Skills

Published May 2017

CONTENTS

Preface

This book is a quick guide to CV building, job search and interview skills.

Before you start applying for jobs read this book from start to finish. This book was written with simplicity and using key terms so you could read quickly and start applying for jobs in the appropriate way. Also this book will establish you with knowledge to enable you answer common interview questions.

When reading this book you will experience a great deal of employability skills and you should continuously make changes. This can include changes to format of your CV, the way you had been applying for jobs, when you should get help from professionals.

You will certainly be successful through reading and applying the skills in this book.

Good luck with your job search.

CHAPTER 1

CLARIFYING YOUR JOB GOALS

Making yourself ready to work should be the first thing to do when looking for employment. This involves making it easier for employers to employ you by demonstrating that you have acquired skills required to do the job through study, voluntary employment, paid work experience or self-employment. Also by demonstrating that you have the ability to learn and develop skills at work. You will also need to be realistic with yourself and give careful thought to work you might do. You should consider duties of a particular job and the skills required for completing given tasks at work. These skills you might already have or you might need to develop by learning from beginning.

To be considered for a particular job, there are some basic skills you should be comfortable with. You should be thoroughly acquainted with particular skills you need so you could get the job you are aiming for. Also you should be able to demonstrate you have skills in handling the duties of the role you are aiming for.

What motivated you to seek employment?

What motivated you to want employment is important and you should spend some time to think about what motivated you. Certainly you will gain from employment and any of the followings are examples of your desire to be in employment; financial independence, making new friends, to keep busy; challenge yourself, enthusiasm.

Getting a voluntary or paid work

Job adverts are drawn up to search for people who have particular skills and qualities. If actually you have the skills and qualities then you will certainly send in your application, on the other hand if you do not have the skills and qualities, you should be in a position where you decide on an achievable job application.

The option available to you is to consider ways to employment that particularly meet your needs. For example a voluntary work could offer you an opportunity where you will be trained in particular skills for a particular line of work. Other option is entry level jobs. These are jobs for people who just finish study and to get these types of jobs you do not require experience. With entry level work you will be trained the skills required to do the job.

Everyone have aspiration to have a job that will allow financial independence. This is your dream job, a job that will allow you to go on holidays, have savings, and meet other financial commitments. Where your skills and qualities are not up to required standard, you should consider getting in employment with career entry job or voluntary work. Chapter three explains this further. You should not confuse part time work with career entry work. People required to do part time work are often highly skilled and experienced as there is no time to train and supervise them as a full time worker.

Research local jobs

You should make research on local jobs available for you to apply for. By finding out the types of jobs available in your local area you will be able to understand where you can get your dream job.

Commuting long distance might be the option for your dream job. Move nearer to where your dream job is to allow you greater chance of getting the job. You might want to do survival jobs to get the money to relocate. You might also want to start voluntary work perhaps for one day a week to be trained and gain experience in the industry you aim to work in. If your job search plan and personal development plan are of standard and well planned you should be able to identify immediate jobs you could do and identify jobs for future may be three to five years' time. This will allow you to plan a career that is achievable starting with jobs available in your local area and onward planning for achieving your dream job.

Be aware of interview questions

To be confident during your interview you need to be aware of the interview questions that will be asked. Also you need to practice answering these questions to enable you to appropriately answer the questions during the interview you are called for. General questions you may be asked at job interview include:

1. **Skills**: the interviewers will want to know you have the ability to do the work. You will be asked questions about your strengths. At this point you should be able to talk about all the skills relevant to the position you are applying for. You might be asked about your weaknesses. At this point you should turn your weaknesses into your strengths. For example you could talk about how your enthusiasm makes you work hard and how you had to be considerate and involve others at completing team tasks.

2. **Qualities**: the interviewers will ask about your qualities that you can bring to the job you are applying for. Here you should be able to list all the qualities of a person that does the job you are applying for. For example the work might require you to be communicative, punctual, trustworthy, committed etc. List the qualities you should have during your answer to the interviewer to be able to write in his/her note. After listing your qualities you should be able to give the interviewer examples of when you have utilised these qualities.

3. **Motivation**: your motivation should be your ambition within the new company you are applying for employment. For example the interviewers may

want to know what motivates you. Your answer need to relate to your ambition within the company such as career progression and promotion within the company. You should be able to give examples how you intend to achieve this also if you have achieved career progression before give examples of activities you did to achieve your career progression at your work. A personal development plan prepared for the interview could be helpful especially when shown to potential employer. Chapter four explains this further. Personal development plan should show how you plan your career within the company you are interested in.

4. **Work history**: interviewers will often ask questions about your previous or current job. They intend to find out about skills you have developed from previous job and how these skills are relevant to the job you are being interviewed for. When answering this question avoid criticising your employer instead answer the question positively and mention skills that are relevant to the job you are being interviewed for and talk about how you are ready to move on to new job and ready to utilise these skills for the job you are being interviewed for.

Also the interviewers may ask questions to find out how you had performed in your previous job. Do not criticise your previous employer, at this point answer the question positively and relate the answers to the skills and qualities the employer want from successful applicant.

5. **Team work**: when the interviewers ask you questions about team work they intend to find out how well you had worked in a team and how you will fit in a new team. You should talk about your first day at work how you initiated team

work. Give examples how you had start off team work at your employment and use key words such as trust and communication.

6. **Ambition**: interviewers may ask questions about your ambition. This is to identify if you have ambition and clear goals within their company. At this point you should give answers that will explain your purpose of applying for the job and how it supports your short term ambition and long term ambition. Remember to make your wishes clear within the company you are applying for.

8. **About the job**: the interviewers may want to find out if you understand the duties of the job you are being interviewed for. For example you might be asked to talk about the roles of the person in the position. You should describe the main duties as it is advertised and how you can perform the duties. This gives assurance to the employer.

9. **The company / employer**: the interviewers may ask you questions about their company. This is to find out about what you had learnt from your research about the company and products or services. Give your answer with skills and sensitivity when making suggestions to the interviewer about their products or services.

10. **Personality and interests**: the interviewer may ask you questions about yourself. This is to find out if you know yourself and what you are good at and where you would like to make improvement.

Learning and developing skills

You may need to learn more about the skills you already have and you may need to develop new skills. It is important for you to meet the requirements of potential employers so learning and developing required skills is important. This will enable you to take part in interview tests and appropriately answer interview questions.

Your job goals are the types of jobs you are looking for. This should be clarified so you do not apply for jobs not matching your skills. Also when your job goals are clarified you will be able to maintain a purposeful learning and development that will enable you to get a job and make career progression while in employment.

You should research the skills associated with the individual types of jobs you are applying for. Make list of the individual skills required for each types of jobs. Identify the skills you already have and skills you need to learn more about and identify skills you need to develop, that is learn from beginners level.

You could advance and develop your skills through volunteering, getting a paid work where they offer learning and development. You can enrol onto a training course specifically designed to improve particular skills you need to advance and develop. When applying for jobs you could mention you would like to take advantage of the offered training in place to further advance and develop your skills.

CHAPTER 2

JOB APPLICATION AND INTERVIEW SKILLS

You should be suitable for a particular vacant job before you put yourself forward as a candidate for the job. Also you need to be prepared before you are called for interview. This removes the tension caused by unpreparedness when the interview letter finally arrives.

Curriculum vitae

You should send your CV for jobs you aim for, the jobs that you had prepared for knowing the likely interview questions and tests, and knowing the skills and qualities of the position. Your CV should always be simple and not complicated to read and for the eyes to follow. It is worth the effort to spend some time to make you CV simple as much as possible. Make your CV simple to read and bearing in mind that people will scan and skim through to find vital information. The contents of your CV should be brief and account for your education, qualifications and work experience.

Be prepared to talk about what you included on your CV including your address and hobbies.

What you should write on your CV include:

1. **Personal details**: your personal details include your name, address, home telephone number, mobile number, email address. Also you can mention social media you are on. Because most employers check social media it is important to update your social media to maintain a professional look. Social media you can join are LinkedIn, Facebook.

Your personal details should include only the ways you would like potential employers to contact you. For example if you would prefer you be contacted by mobile phone number, then you do not need to include your home number. Also avoid private information such as your age, date of birth, nationality, national insurance number, marital status.

2. **Personal profile**: your personal profile is your advert on your CV. This should include your skills and qualities, your experience and achievements, your career aims.

Your personal profile should be simple, that is easily understood and uncomplicated. Try scan and skim reading your personal profile and make changes.

3. **Employment history**: your employment history should start form the most current or most recent job and list them backwards till you reach your last job. You should include in your job history date, employer's name, job title, and main role. The relevant jobs to your application should be more detailed. Here you can include your duties and achievements.

Avoid gaps in your employment history and list your history briefly and in details when relevant to the job you are applying for.

4. **Education**: your education section should be listed starting from the most recent education and listed backwards. This should include date, name of college / university, and achievement.

5. **Interests**: your interests should include your informal activities. This is an opportunity to appeal to the senses of the person reading your CV. This should show your passion for socialising with people.

6. **References**: you do not need to write the details of your references. You can write 'References available on request'.

Cover letter

Your cover letter should be simple and not long letter. Address the letter to the named person on the advert. Your cover letter should be straight to the point and persuading.

Your cover letter should include your skills. Explain how your skills match the role you are applying for. Also include your qualities and explain how your qualities are the qualities the employer are looking for. Talk about transferable skills from work you had done, comparing your skills to skills the employer are looking for. Remember to sign and date your cover letter.

Personal statement

When applying for a job that required completing an application form you need to complete the application form as expected by the company. The company had designed the application form in order to collect the same information from candidates, and use the consistent information during screening process.

The vital part of an application form is the personal statement section. The presentation of the answers in your personal statement should be presented with consistent format. Also you should provide evidence within your answers. You do not necessarily have to give answer to all the questions. Ensure that the ones you answered are presented to a very high standard.

To present your personal statement with consistency you can use the STAR technique. This is Situation – description of the situation; Task – task to be completed; Actions – what you did or actions that resolved an issue; Results – the results of your actions.

Also begin and end your personal statement in a formal letter format.

Interview

You should always be prepared for your interview. This is an oral examination of your suitability for the job you applied for. Be prepared to present your information in a meaningful way by building the knowledge of possible questions as explained in chapter one. The possible questions will always be based on the skills and qualities of a person for the role you are applying for. Also be prepared for test, often to be taken before your interview. The test could be on different day to the interview and it could be on the same day of the interview. Often the test is based on the skills you will need to apply at work regarding use of English, Maths and ICT. The test can also be based solely on knowledge of particular skills relating to the job you are applying for. If you are going to be using a great deal of skills relating to English, Maths and ICT or any particular skills at work, be sure you are able pass the test by undergoing learning and development.

During an interview you will be asked questions relating to necessary skills and qualities required to carry out the duties of the position. You should be very comfortable to answer questions about the skills and qualities necessary to carry out the duties of the position you are being interviewed for. When your answers are accurate and correct the interview will seem quick, enjoyable and memorable to you and the interviewer. When the interviewer remembered your interview, this will start the process of being considered.

When answering interview questions you can use the STAR technique to present your answers.

Types of CVs

Experience or education should be written first on your CV after your details and personal profile. This depends on your level of experience. If your experience is more work related or educational related. Your stronger point of experience should be written first.

The types of CV include:

1. **Chronological CV**: chronological CV is the most common type of CV. Particular attention is given to list the experience in a chronological order on the CV in the order from which they occur starting from the most recent.

Chronological CV is often preferred by employers. It is suitable when you are applying for jobs in the same sector because it easily shows your progression.

The format for chronological CV should include:

Personal details

Personal profile

Employment history

Education

Interests

References

2. **Functional CV**: functional CV is common when applying for executive jobs. Particular attention is given to your achievements, skills and qualities.

Functional CV is suitable if you have gaps in your career or you are changing career. This is because it draws employers' attention to your transferable skills.

The format for functional CV should include:

Personal details

Personal profile

Sections on skills and abilities

Employment history (outlined)

Education

3. **Combined CV**: combined CV is becoming popular; it is combination of both chronological CV and functional CV.

The format for combined CV should include:

Personal details

Personal profile

Sections on skills and abilities

Employment history (detailed)

Education

Types of cover letters

Your cover letter should be formal, dated, and signed. You need to write in an appropriate way. You should do this by choosing the correct type of cover letter depending on the fact you are either applying directly in response to an advert or seeking help in job search. You should use the appropriate cover letter for the application you are making.

Types of cover letters include:

1. **Application cover letter**: you should write an application cover letter for jobs advertised, this is a specific response to a vacant job. The letter should show your interest in working for the company.

2. **Prospecting cover letter**: you should write a prospecting cover letter when you are making inquiry. Your letter should ask for job opening from a company

you wish to work for. The letter should show your interest in working in the sector.

3. **Networking cover letter**: you should write networking cover letter when you wanted to market yourself. Asking friends and friends of friends to introduce you to job openings, give you advice as to where to search for jobs.

Types of interviews

Types of interviews you could be called for varies and you should be prepared for them. You could also ask an organisation for details about the type of interview they are using and if there will be test.

Types of interviews include:

1. **Face-to-face interview**: you could be asked for a direct personal contact interview. This is in person and the most popular type of interview.

2. **Telephone interview**: you could be telephoned for an interview. Ideally the interviewer would arrange a suitable time with you either by email or telephone call. You should arrange earliest possible time for the telephone interview to take place.

The interviewer might want interview to take place on first time you were telephoned. You should bear in mind that telephone interview is often used when there is not enough time for screening candidates so it is important that you are confident with the skills and qualities required to do the job before you send in your application.

Also this type of interview is often used where the job involved using the telephone.

3. **Video interview**: you could be asked for a video interview where you can see each other and hear each other from different locations. This is often done via Skype.

4. **Competency-based interview**: you could be asked for competency-based interview. The questions will be about your skills and qualities.

5. **Technical interview**: when you are asked for technical type of interview, you will be asked to demonstrate your skills while being observed.

6. **Panel interview**: you could be asked for panel interview where panel of interviewers will be asking you questions. One panel member leads the interviewers and questions will be asked in turns.

7. **Informal chat interview**: your interview could be informal interview. You should have discussion about your suitability in an informal way. Informal type of interview is often used in creative industry.

8. **Group discussion interview**: you could be asked for group discussion interview where other candidates for the job will be present. You should be

able to respect others and allow others to have their turn to speak. You will be observed how you present yourself in a team and your determination to get the job.

Customising your CV and cover letter

You should always change your CV and cover letter to make them relevant to the job you are applying for. This will allow your CV and cover letter to stand out from the crowd. Also it will allow your CV and cover letter to be found in the automated screening system.

When customising your CV and cover letter use key words from the advertised job. Also use the job's key words for skills and qualities.

Job search methods

You should know the ways to search the labour market for suitable jobs. When you search for jobs in a careful and thorough way using one or combination of the job search methods, you will certainly get a job you had determined to get.

The ways to search for jobs include:

1. **Internet**: the internet has vast number of jobs and it can be overwhelming to sift through. You should determine the types of jobs you would apply for to make it easier to use the internet to search for jobs. You could go directly to job searching on particular industry website for job seekers and directly to a company's website and search for suitable jobs.

2. **Professional associations**: professional associations that relate to the types of jobs you are looking for often have job opportunities section often used by members of the association to advertise job vacancies. You could use the professional associations to search for jobs via their magazines and websites.

3. **Networking**: you could use the network of friends and friends of friends to ask for information about vacancies and to circulate your CV.

4. **Career fairs**: you could attend job fairs to meet potential employers. This is an opportunity to meet potential employers and network.

5. **Company websites**: you could visit company of interest's websites to search for vacant position. Company websites provide job seekers particular information to follow for making job application to their company.

6. **Employment agencies**: you could find employment agencies that offer the types of jobs you are looking for and sign contract with them.

7. **Cold calling**: cold calling is contacting potential employers to ask if they have job that is suitable for you. You should be prepared before making the call because it can be at first intimidating. With enough practice you should be ready to make cold calling. You need to research the company before making cold calling.

8. **Newspapers and magazines**: newspapers and magazines although one of the oldest way of looking for job. It is still useful to look into local newspapers and magazines. This will provide you opportunity to view the types of jobs in your local area.

Getting ready for interview

Interviewers would want to hold discussion with you to see if you are the right person for the job. The chance you have to discuss well is important so you should be prepared and know the likely questions. You need to make it easy for you to perform well in an interview by preparing for the interview you are called for. You should be able to anticipate the likely interview questions and be prepared for appropriate answers by familiarising yourself with the best way to respond to the question. The way to do this is to be well informed and up to date with the skills, qualities, experience, knowledge required to do the duties of the job.

What you should do to get ready for an interview include:

1. **Get a bag for your interviews**: get a bag for your interviews and in this bag keep all the things your will need for your interviews. This makes it easier and time saving to organise everything you need when called for an interview.

2. **Plan and prepare what you will wear**: do not leave preparing what you will wear to the day of the interview. Planning and preparing what you will wear can be time consuming. Dress professionally for the interview. Also wear dress you are comfortable in.

3. **Plan your journey**: you should plan your journey by looking up the train and bus timetable and time to walk. Also give time for alternative route to your interview and time for train and bus delays. Find the nearest café shop that you can use before and after your interview.

4. **Sleep well**: be organised by preparing and planning for an interview so you can have enough time to sleep well before the interview day.

5. **Research the company**: research the company's products or services and how the vacant job's duties fit into the company goals. Also research the terminologies that will be appropriate to use in the interview.

Assessing your interview performance

Assessing your interview performance is important because it will allow you to prepare yourself for the result of the interview. It will also give you second chance to clarify concerns about your interview where the interviewers decided to telephone you or ask you for a second interview. Also it allows you to learn from the interview where you need to improve.

Think about the feedback given you after your interview. If you successfully get the job or not you should use the feedback to improve on your future performance; either at work area where you are believed to have performed well at the interview or at another interview.

CHAPTER 3

UNDERSTAND AVAILABLE WAYS INTO LABOUR MARKET

Labour market

The labour market is formed of supply of labour and demand of labour. You should be aware that not everyone is in the labour market for some reason. This can be because they are not available or they do not have required skills and experience. The labour market is a place where people available for work come to compete for best suitable jobs and where employers come to compete to hire the best worker available to work.

Available ways to get into the labour market

In order to get into the labour market you will need certain skills and experience. There are various ways to make yourself available for employment. You can consider being available for employment as you having the necessary skills and experience to do certain work and being available for work. In the case where you have not got necessary skills and experience there are ways to build your skills and experience.

You should look into variety of ways into labour market and select the one that is appropriate for the type of career you aim for. Some ways into labour market will provide you with practice in technical jobs such as construction job or computer engineering.

The available ways to get into the labour market include:

1. **Volunteering**: you could volunteer your service to an organisation in order to be trained and gain experience required for the labour market. Often organisations provide learning and development opportunities for people who are volunteering with them. When you participate in an organisation's learning and development opportunities you will gain vital skills and experience that will allow you to be able to compete for available jobs in the labour market.

There are volunteer jobs out there that offer to train applicants and there are volunteer roles for people who are skilled and experienced. You might be out of paid work for some reasons. You should use the spare time not currently in use to volunteer for an organisation in order not to have gaps in your CV. Employers will be delighted to hire someone who have no gaps in their CV and constructively utilised their time while out of paid work.

Other voluntary work can involve working in the family either caring for someone or working in the family business. These also are unpaid work that you could do in order to gain skills and experience.

You should search for volunteer roles on websites that are specifically for voluntary roles. The websites for the labour market where employers are searching for skilled workers do not often have voluntary jobs. It is important to search dedicated websites. Also some organisations in your local area are dedicated to finding voluntary roles for applicants. You should use such organisations and their facilities to get voluntary work.

2. **Self-employment**: you could work for yourself instead of an employer as a freelance or owner of a business in order to gain valuable skills and experience needed to get into the labour market. The experience you could gain will be helpful for you to getting paid employment in the future.

Self-employment is often suitable for older people who are out of job for some reason and wanted to fill the gap in their CV by setting up their own business. Older people are more likely to start a business and run it successfully than younger people because they already have the skills, specialties and finance required to start a business. If you are young and sure about your business potential and have a realistic business plan, you should take advantage of the opportunity and start your own business. The skills and experience you will gain will be highly valuable to potential employers.

The government support people to set up their own business. You should find out about the support available in your local area. The supports can be for drawing up your business plan and having someone for mentor or consultation. The support can also be in the form of financial support offered to people starting their own business.

3. **Study programmes**: study programme is a way of building skills and experience for a given career. Your work at the college or university will often include essay writing, tests and simulated work experience or work placement. These are the kinds of experience employers are looking for.

Also you should find employment while you are studying. There are many part time jobs that will add value to your study. Part-time jobs are for only part of the usual working day or week. Also voluntary work is another way to build skills and experience in your area of study while at the college or university. Employers will be delighted to hire someone who have had paid or voluntary work experience that is related to what they studied at the college or university.

Colleges and universities have career department. You should use the college or university's career department for searching for part-time jobs or voluntary jobs while you are at the college or university.

Some courses require you to go on work experience as a project to be completed as part of the course. You can find a course that required you to go on work experience where you will complete a project while working. This adds value to your CV because employers often are looking for candidates who are qualified and experienced.

4. **Work placement**: work placement is temporary posting of someone in a workplace to gain work experience. You can either go on a work placement through your college or find a work placement on your own while studying. When finding work placement on your own you can use the college or university you are in to assist you in your search. Your college or university may be able to write you a work placement letter to send along with your application to potential employers.

When searching college or university for a course, you should search for courses that match your job goals and search for opportunities for work placement arranged by the college or university. The work placement will put you at work where you will be working along people who are in the industry for some time. You will be supervised and may have a mentor who will give you advice and instruct you on how to complete tasks at work.

Working along people in the industry is an opportunity to gain vital work experience. You should use the opportunity to your advantage.

Also you should search for vacancies while you are at the work placement via the company's website and HR department. Also there are jobs that are for internal staff that are not advertised. Finding out about available jobs and the company's recruitment process could earn you a dream job.

5. **Gap year**: gap year is a period of time usually a year taken by a student as a break from college or university. You should use your gap year wisely and take up work that is related to what you are studying at the college or university.

Employers will be impressed when you take up a job that is related to the course you studied at the university, because of this it is advisable to do something that is relevant to the course you are studying.

6. **Apprenticeships**: apprenticeship is a work training period where you will be learning a trade from a skilled employer and being paid while you are working.

Many organisations advertise apprenticeship opportunities, also you should search websites of organisations you are interested in and find information about their apprenticeship jobs.

7. **Traineeships**: traineeship is a course with time spent learning skills under supervision of an employer. You will spend time at college and at work learning the skills required to do a particular type of job.

CHAPTER 4

JOB SEARCH PLAN AND PERSONAL DEVELOPMENT PLAN

Job search plan

Getting any job in the industry you are interested in is important as much as getting a specific job you are interested in. This is because you can follow career progression once you are in an organisation. You should know how to search for jobs in a specific industry and how to maintain a personal development plan. It is important to understand that you can start your career from lower paid work or even voluntary work and walk your way up the employment ladder till you get your dream job.

You could follow the following steps to job search plan to finding your dream jobs or alternative jobs you could do in an industry.

Job search plan steps should include:

1. **Type of work**: you should research between one to five different types of jobs you are interested in. Research the skills required to do the jobs, research qualities of the person that does the jobs, research their educational requirement, and research expected pay in the industry for the jobs.

2. **Career potential**: for each of the five jobs listed, write the potential for future career while doing such type of job. For example possible promotion within a company also skills you could use for other jobs listed.

3. **Prepare your CV and cover letter**: prepare appropriate CV and cover letter. Use results of your research to put important key words, skills and qualities on your CV. This will make your CV searchable by potential employer's automated screening process and make your CV impressive.

Also write the appropriate cover letter to send along with your CV to potential employers.

4. **Get organised**: get organised before you start sending out your CV or making contact with potential employers. Employers sometimes respond quickly to job application so you are expected to be organised. What you need to do include, familiarising yourself with content of your CV and cover letter, prepare your references, have written references ready, organise your certificates. Have all your documents in electronic form in USB and hard copy. Ideally have all your documents and USB in your dedicated bag for interview.

5. **Contact employers**: contact potential employers using employment agencies, online vacancies, and newspapers. You can also research and contact a particular organisation you are interested in.

6. **Keep records**: maintain records of contacts with potential employers. Record their feedback from interview. Record the next step to take to prepare for career progression when offered the job or record what you have learnt from the interview and the next step to take in preparation for the next interview.

Personal development plan

Personal development plan is reflection and action plan. Personal development plan can be drawn up for yourself for your career while you are searching for work or while you are employed. While searching for work or at work you could complete a personal development plan to advance your career this would help you to keep abreast of developments that are happening in your line of work.

Ask potential employers for duties and person specification of a particular job you have interest in or had applied for or been ask for an interview. You should build a personal development plan using the information provided to you. You could give copy to your interviewers, they will be impressed with what you can do and areas you plan further learning and development. If your personal development plan is of high standard, this would really impress potential employers and they would want to further discuss your personal development plan while you are employed with them.

The steps to draw up personal development plan for future job include:

1. Identify requirements of your future role.
2. Identify your strengths, areas for further development, opportunities and threats.
3. Complete a SMART action plan
4. Complete your personal objectives.

Identify requirements of your future job

You could look in the person specification to identify requirements of future roles or look in the advertised job. This can include key task, knowledge and understanding, people you will be working with as a team and external links etc.

Having identified requirements of your future role, create a form as below and make a list:

Requirements of my future role:

1.	
2.	
3.	
4.	

Identify your strengths, areas for further development, opportunities and threats

Make a personal analysis of yourself drawing on your experience. Your experience may be from education, voluntary work, or paid work. This will give you the opportunity to reflect on the list you had made from above. Also this will make you aware of your strength and weaknesses.

Create a personal analysis form as below and complete your personal analysis table:

Strengths	Areas for further development
Opportunities	Threats

Complete a SMART action plan

Create an action plan as below. Your action plan should be SMART. That is Specific, Measurable, Attainable, Relevant, and Time-bound.

What I want to learn.	What I have to do.	Support and resources I would need.	How I will measure success.	Target completion date and review.

Complete your personal objectives

Complete personal objectives as below showing your short term goal, medium term goal and long term goal

Short term goals (12 months)
Medium term goals (2 – 3 years)
Long term goals (3 years and beyond)

Questions will be asked on most of the items on your personal development plan so it is important to complete one before going to an interview.

While in employment personal development plan can be used to either improve your efficiency at work or gain promotion.

Personal development plan should be reviewed regularly in order to complete its cycle.